50 Hawaiian Vacation Recipes for Home

By: Kelly Johnson

Table of Contents

- Kalua Pork
- Loco Moco
- Huli Huli Chicken
- Ahi Poke Bowl
- Haupia (Coconut Pudding)
- Spam Musubi
- Pineapple Fried Rice
- Poi Pancakes
- Lū'au Chicken
- Macadamia Nut Crusted Mahi Mahi
- Teriyaki Beef Skewers
- Hawaiian Sweet Rolls
- Shoyu Chicken
- Lomi Lomi Salmon
- Hawaiian Garlic Shrimp
- Lau Lau
- Mango BBQ Ribs
- Taro Chips with Pineapple Salsa
- Pupus (Appetizer Platter)
- Coconut Shrimp
- Malasadas (Portuguese Doughnuts)
- Huli Huli Tofu Skewers
- Mochiko Chicken
- Pineapple Upside-Down Cake
- Hawaiian Plate Lunch
- Banana Macadamia Nut Bread
- Ahi Tuna Tacos
- Hawaiian Pizza
- Loco Moco Burger
- Coconut Shrimp Tacos
- Hawaiian BBQ Meatballs
- Pineapple Coconut Smoothie Bowl
- Hawaiian Style BBQ Pulled Pork Sliders
- Huli Huli Tempeh Bowl
- Grilled Pineapple with Honey Lime Glaze

- Huli Huli Veggie Skewers
- Mango Coconut Ice Cream
- Pineapple Teriyaki Veggie Burgers
- Hawaiian Chicken Salad
- Taro Bubble Tea
- Coconut Tapioca Pudding
- Hawaiian Breakfast Sandwich
- Haupia Pie
- Pineapple Coconut Cake
- Ahi Poke Nachos
- Taro Pancakes with Coconut Syrup
- Hawaiian Macaroni Salad
- Lū'au Punch
- Grilled Pineapple Slices with Cinnamon Sugar
- Hawaiian Shaved Ice with Tropical Fruit Syrup

Kalua Pork

Ingredients:

- 4-5 lbs pork shoulder or pork butt, boneless
- 1 tablespoon liquid smoke
- 1 tablespoon sea salt or Hawaiian salt
- 1 tablespoon garlic powder
- 1 tablespoon onion powder
- 1 teaspoon ground black pepper

Instructions:

1. Pierce the pork all over with a fork to allow the flavors to penetrate.
2. Rub the liquid smoke all over the pork.
3. In a small bowl, mix together the sea salt, garlic powder, onion powder, and black pepper to make the seasoning rub.
4. Rub the seasoning mixture all over the pork, ensuring it's evenly coated.
5. If using a slow cooker, place the seasoned pork in the slow cooker and cook on low for 8-10 hours or on high for 4-6 hours, until the pork is very tender and easily falls apart.
6. If using an oven, preheat the oven to 325°F (160°C). Place the seasoned pork in a roasting pan or Dutch oven, cover tightly with foil or a lid, and roast for about 4-5 hours, until the pork is fork-tender.
7. Once the pork is cooked, remove it from the slow cooker or oven and let it rest for a few minutes.
8. Shred the pork using two forks or chop it into chunks.
9. Serve the Kalua Pork hot with steamed white rice and your favorite side dishes, such as macaroni salad or cabbage slaw.
10. Enjoy your delicious homemade Kalua Pork!

This recipe captures the smoky, savory flavors of traditional Kalua Pork, making it a perfect dish for a Hawaiian-inspired meal at home.

Loco Moco

Ingredients:

- 1 lb ground beef
- Salt and pepper, to taste
- 4 cups cooked white rice
- 4 large eggs
- 2 cups beef gravy (store-bought or homemade)
- Optional: chopped green onions for garnish

Instructions:

1. Divide the ground beef into four equal portions and shape them into thick hamburger patties. Season both sides of the patties with salt and pepper.
2. Heat a skillet or griddle over medium-high heat. Cook the hamburger patties for about 4-5 minutes per side, or until they are cooked through and nicely browned. Remove them from the skillet and set aside.
3. In the same skillet, fry the eggs sunny-side up or to your desired doneness.
4. While the eggs are cooking, warm the beef gravy in a saucepan over low heat.
5. To assemble the Loco Moco bowls, divide the cooked rice among four serving bowls.
6. Place a cooked hamburger patty on top of each mound of rice.
7. Carefully place a fried egg on top of each hamburger patty.
8. Spoon warm beef gravy generously over the eggs and patties.
9. Garnish with chopped green onions, if desired.
10. Serve the Loco Moco immediately, while still hot, and enjoy!

Feel free to customize your Loco Moco by adding extra toppings like sautéed onions, mushrooms, or even a sprinkle of furikake for extra flavor. It's a delicious and filling dish that's sure to become a favorite!

Huli Huli Chicken

Ingredients:

For the marinade:

- 1/2 cup soy sauce
- 1/2 cup pineapple juice
- 1/4 cup brown sugar
- 1/4 cup ketchup
- 2 tablespoons rice vinegar
- 2 cloves garlic, minced
- 1 teaspoon grated fresh ginger
- 1 teaspoon sesame oil
- 1/4 teaspoon black pepper

For the chicken:

- 4 boneless, skinless chicken breasts or chicken thighs
- Optional: sliced green onions and sesame seeds for garnish

Instructions:

1. In a mixing bowl, whisk together all the marinade ingredients until well combined.
2. Place the chicken breasts or thighs in a large resealable plastic bag or a shallow dish.
3. Pour the marinade over the chicken, making sure it's evenly coated. Seal the bag or cover the dish and refrigerate for at least 2 hours, or preferably overnight, to allow the flavors to meld.
4. Preheat your grill to medium-high heat (about 375-400°F / 190-200°C) and lightly oil the grates to prevent sticking.
5. Remove the chicken from the marinade and discard any excess marinade.
6. Grill the chicken for 6-8 minutes per side, or until fully cooked through, with an internal temperature of 165°F (74°C) for chicken breasts or 175°F (80°C) for chicken thighs.
7. While grilling, you can baste the chicken with additional marinade to keep it moist and add extra flavor.

8. Once the chicken is cooked through and nicely charred on the outside, remove it from the grill and let it rest for a few minutes before serving.
9. Optionally, garnish the Huli Huli Chicken with sliced green onions and sesame seeds for a decorative touch.
10. Serve the Huli Huli Chicken hot with your favorite side dishes, such as rice, grilled pineapple, or a fresh salad.
11. Enjoy your homemade Huli Huli Chicken, reminiscent of the flavors of Hawaii!

Ahi Poke Bowl

Ingredients:

For the poke:

- 1 lb sushi-grade ahi tuna, cut into bite-sized cubes
- 1/4 cup soy sauce
- 1 tablespoon sesame oil
- 1 tablespoon rice vinegar
- 1 teaspoon grated fresh ginger
- 1 teaspoon minced garlic
- 1 teaspoon honey or brown sugar
- 2 green onions, thinly sliced
- Optional: sesame seeds, chopped cilantro, sliced avocado for garnish

For the bowl:

- 4 cups cooked sushi rice or jasmine rice
- Toppings of your choice: sliced cucumber, shredded carrots, edamame, sliced radishes, avocado, seaweed salad, pickled ginger, wasabi, etc.

Instructions:

1. In a mixing bowl, whisk together the soy sauce, sesame oil, rice vinegar, ginger, garlic, and honey until well combined to make the marinade.
2. Add the cubed ahi tuna to the marinade and gently toss to coat. Cover the bowl and refrigerate for at least 30 minutes to allow the flavors to meld.
3. While the tuna is marinating, prepare the rice according to package instructions. Once cooked, let the rice cool slightly before assembling the poke bowls.
4. To assemble the poke bowls, divide the cooked rice among serving bowls.
5. Top each bowl of rice with a portion of the marinated ahi tuna.
6. Arrange your desired toppings around the tuna on each bowl.
7. Garnish the poke bowls with sliced green onions, sesame seeds, chopped cilantro, and sliced avocado, if desired.
8. Serve the poke bowls immediately, and enjoy!

Feel free to customize your Ahi Poke Bowls with your favorite toppings and additional sauces, such as spicy mayo or sriracha aioli, for extra flavor. It's a fresh and vibrant dish that's perfect for a taste of Hawaii at home!

Haupia (Coconut Pudding)

Ingredients:

- 2 cups coconut milk
- 1/2 cup sugar
- 1/2 cup water
- 1/2 cup cornstarch
- Optional: shredded coconut for garnish

Instructions:

1. In a medium saucepan, combine the coconut milk, sugar, and water over medium heat. Stir until the sugar is dissolved and the mixture is well combined.
2. In a small bowl, mix the cornstarch with a small amount of water to create a slurry, ensuring there are no lumps.
3. Slowly pour the cornstarch slurry into the coconut milk mixture, whisking continuously to prevent lumps from forming.
4. Cook the mixture over medium heat, stirring constantly, until it thickens and resembles pudding consistency, about 5-7 minutes.
5. Once the mixture has thickened, remove it from the heat and pour it into a shallow dish or individual serving cups.
6. Allow the Haupia to cool at room temperature for a few minutes, then refrigerate for at least 2 hours, or until set.
7. Once chilled and set, slice the Haupia into squares or scoop it into individual servings.
8. Optionally, garnish each serving with shredded coconut for added texture and flavor.
9. Serve the Haupia chilled and enjoy its creamy coconut goodness!

Haupia is a simple yet delicious dessert that's sure to be a hit with coconut lovers. It's perfect for serving at tropical-themed parties or anytime you want to add a taste of Hawaii to your dessert menu.

Spam Musubi

Ingredients:

- 1 can of Spam
- 2 cups cooked sushi rice (short-grain rice)
- 2 sheets of nori (seaweed), cut into strips
- Soy sauce
- Sugar
- Furikake (optional)
- Cooking oil (for frying)

Instructions:

1. Slice the Spam into 8 equal slices. You can adjust the thickness of the slices according to your preference.
2. In a small bowl, mix together 2 tablespoons of soy sauce and 1 tablespoon of sugar to make the marinade.
3. Place the Spam slices in a shallow dish or resealable plastic bag and pour the marinade over them. Ensure each slice is coated evenly. Let them marinate for about 15-30 minutes.
4. While the Spam is marinating, prepare the sushi rice according to package instructions. Once cooked, let the rice cool slightly so it's easier to handle.
5. Heat a non-stick skillet or frying pan over medium heat. Add a small amount of cooking oil to the pan.
6. Place the marinated Spam slices in the pan and fry them for about 2-3 minutes on each side, or until they are lightly browned and caramelized. Remove them from the pan and set aside.
7. To assemble the Spam Musubi, place a musubi mold (or use clean hands) on a flat surface. Lay a strip of nori on the bottom of the mold.
8. Fill the mold with a layer of rice, pressing it down gently to pack it together.
9. Place a slice of cooked Spam on top of the rice in the mold.
10. Add another layer of rice on top of the Spam, pressing it down gently to pack it together.
11. Use the musubi mold to press the rice and Spam together firmly into a rectangular shape.
12. Carefully remove the mold, leaving the assembled Spam Musubi behind.

13. Wrap the strip of nori around the Spam Musubi, sealing the edges by moistening them slightly with water.
14. Repeat the process with the remaining Spam slices and rice to make additional Spam Musubi.
15. Optionally, sprinkle some furikake over the top of each Spam Musubi for added flavor.
16. Serve the Spam Musubi immediately, or wrap them individually in plastic wrap for later enjoyment.

Spam Musubi is a delicious and portable snack that's perfect for picnics, lunchboxes, or anytime you're craving a taste of Hawaii! Enjoy!

Pineapple Fried Rice

Ingredients:

- 3 cups cooked jasmine rice (preferably chilled)
- 2 tablespoons vegetable oil
- 2 cloves garlic, minced
- 1 small onion, diced
- 1 bell pepper, diced (any color)
- 1 carrot, diced
- 1 cup diced pineapple (fresh or canned)
- 1 cup frozen peas, thawed
- 2 green onions, chopped
- 2 tablespoons soy sauce
- 1 tablespoon fish sauce (optional, for added umami flavor)
- 1 tablespoon curry powder
- 1/2 teaspoon turmeric powder (optional, for color)
- Salt and pepper, to taste
- Optional protein: cooked shrimp, chicken, or tofu

Instructions:

1. Heat the vegetable oil in a large skillet or wok over medium-high heat.
2. Add the minced garlic and diced onion to the skillet and sauté for 2-3 minutes, or until fragrant and translucent.
3. Add the diced bell pepper and carrot to the skillet and cook for an additional 2-3 minutes, or until the vegetables are slightly softened.
4. Push the vegetables to one side of the skillet and add the cooked protein (if using) to the empty side. Cook for 2-3 minutes, or until heated through.
5. Add the chilled cooked rice to the skillet, breaking up any clumps with a spatula. Stir-fry the rice with the vegetables and protein for 3-4 minutes, or until the rice is heated through and starting to turn golden.
6. Add the diced pineapple and thawed peas to the skillet, and continue to stir-fry for another 2-3 minutes.
7. In a small bowl, mix together the soy sauce, fish sauce (if using), curry powder, and turmeric powder.
8. Pour the sauce mixture over the fried rice in the skillet and toss everything together until well combined.

9. Season the Pineapple Fried Rice with salt and pepper to taste, adjusting the seasoning as needed.
10. Stir in the chopped green onions and cook for another minute.
11. Remove the skillet from the heat and transfer the Pineapple Fried Rice to a serving dish.
12. Serve the Pineapple Fried Rice hot as a delicious main dish or side dish, garnished with additional chopped green onions or fresh cilantro if desired.

Enjoy your homemade Pineapple Fried Rice, packed with vibrant flavors and colorful ingredients!

Poi Pancakes

Ingredients:

- 1 cup all-purpose flour
- 1 tablespoon sugar
- 1 teaspoon baking powder
- 1/2 teaspoon baking soda
- 1/4 teaspoon salt
- 1/2 cup poi (fresh or thawed if frozen)
- 1 cup buttermilk
- 1 large egg
- 2 tablespoons melted butter or vegetable oil
- Butter or oil for cooking
- Optional toppings: sliced bananas, berries, coconut flakes, maple syrup

Instructions:

1. In a large mixing bowl, whisk together the flour, sugar, baking powder, baking soda, and salt until well combined.
2. In a separate bowl, whisk together the poi, buttermilk, egg, and melted butter or oil until smooth.
3. Pour the wet ingredients into the dry ingredients and stir until just combined. Be careful not to overmix; a few lumps are okay.
4. Heat a non-stick skillet or griddle over medium heat and lightly grease with butter or oil.
5. Pour about 1/4 cup of batter onto the skillet for each pancake. Use the back of a spoon or a spatula to spread the batter into a round shape, if necessary.
6. Cook the pancakes for 2-3 minutes, or until bubbles form on the surface and the edges look set.
7. Flip the pancakes and cook for an additional 1-2 minutes on the other side, or until golden brown and cooked through.
8. Repeat with the remaining batter, greasing the skillet as needed between batches.
9. Serve the Poi Pancakes hot with your favorite toppings, such as sliced bananas, berries, coconut flakes, or maple syrup.
10. Enjoy your delicious and unique Poi Pancakes, showcasing the flavors of Hawaii!

These pancakes are a delightful way to incorporate the flavors of Hawaii into your breakfast routine. They're fluffy, flavorful, and perfect for a leisurely weekend brunch.

Lū'au Chicken

Ingredients:

- 4 boneless, skinless chicken breasts or thighs
- Salt and pepper, to taste
- 2 tablespoons vegetable oil
- 1 onion, chopped
- 2 cloves garlic, minced
- 1 tablespoon grated fresh ginger
- 1 can (14 ounces) coconut milk
- 1/4 cup soy sauce
- 2 tablespoons brown sugar
- 1 tablespoon rice vinegar
- 1 tablespoon cornstarch
- 2 cups fresh spinach leaves
- Cooked white rice, for serving

Instructions:

1. Season the chicken breasts or thighs with salt and pepper on both sides.
2. Heat the vegetable oil in a large skillet or Dutch oven over medium-high heat.
3. Add the seasoned chicken to the skillet and cook for 4-5 minutes on each side, or until browned and cooked through. Remove the chicken from the skillet and set aside.
4. In the same skillet, add the chopped onion, minced garlic, and grated ginger. Sauté for 2-3 minutes, or until fragrant and softened.
5. In a small bowl, whisk together the coconut milk, soy sauce, brown sugar, rice vinegar, and cornstarch until smooth.
6. Pour the coconut milk mixture into the skillet with the onions, garlic, and ginger. Stir well to combine.
7. Bring the mixture to a simmer and cook for 3-4 minutes, or until slightly thickened.
8. Return the cooked chicken to the skillet, nestling it into the sauce. Cover and simmer for an additional 5-7 minutes, or until the chicken is heated through and the sauce has thickened further.
9. Stir in the fresh spinach leaves and cook for 1-2 minutes, or until wilted.
10. Serve the Lū'au Chicken hot over cooked white rice.

11. Enjoy your homemade Lū'au Chicken, a delicious taste of Hawaiian cuisine!

This dish is perfect for a Hawaiian-themed dinner or anytime you're craving a flavorful and comforting meal.

Macadamia Nut Crusted Mahi Mahi

Ingredients:

- 4 mahi mahi fillets (about 6 ounces each)
- Salt and pepper, to taste
- 1 cup macadamia nuts, finely chopped or crushed
- 1/2 cup panko breadcrumbs
- 1/4 cup all-purpose flour
- 2 eggs, beaten
- 2 tablespoons olive oil or melted butter

Optional sauce:

- 1/4 cup mayonnaise
- 1 tablespoon lime juice
- 1 teaspoon honey
- 1 teaspoon Dijon mustard
- Salt and pepper, to taste

Instructions:

1. Preheat your oven to 375°F (190°C). Line a baking sheet with parchment paper or lightly grease it with cooking spray.
2. Season the mahi mahi fillets with salt and pepper on both sides.
3. In a shallow dish, combine the finely chopped macadamia nuts, panko breadcrumbs, and a pinch of salt and pepper.
4. Place the flour in another shallow dish, and the beaten eggs in a third shallow dish.
5. Dredge each mahi mahi fillet in the flour, shaking off any excess.
6. Dip each floured fillet into the beaten eggs, ensuring it's coated evenly.
7. Press each fillet into the macadamia nut mixture, coating it thoroughly on both sides.
8. Place the coated mahi mahi fillets on the prepared baking sheet.
9. Drizzle olive oil or melted butter over the top of each fillet to help them brown and crisp up.

10. Bake the Macadamia Nut Crusted Mahi Mahi in the preheated oven for 12-15 minutes, or until the fish is cooked through and the crust is golden brown and crispy.
11. While the fish is baking, you can prepare the optional sauce by whisking together the mayonnaise, lime juice, honey, Dijon mustard, salt, and pepper in a small bowl. Adjust the seasoning to taste.
12. Once the Mahi Mahi is cooked, remove it from the oven and let it rest for a few minutes before serving.
13. Serve the Macadamia Nut Crusted Mahi Mahi hot, garnished with fresh herbs and accompanied by the optional sauce on the side.
14. Enjoy your delicious and flavorful Macadamia Nut Crusted Mahi Mahi!

This dish pairs wonderfully with steamed vegetables, rice, or a fresh salad for a complete meal.

Teriyaki Beef Skewers

Ingredients:

- 1 lb beef steak (such as sirloin or flank), thinly sliced against the grain
- Salt and pepper, to taste
- Wooden or metal skewers (if using wooden skewers, soak them in water for 30 minutes before grilling)
- Sesame seeds and chopped green onions, for garnish (optional)

For the teriyaki marinade:

- 1/2 cup soy sauce
- 1/4 cup mirin (Japanese sweet rice wine)
- 2 tablespoons honey or brown sugar
- 2 tablespoons rice vinegar
- 2 cloves garlic, minced
- 1 teaspoon grated fresh ginger
- 1 tablespoon cornstarch
- 2 tablespoons water

Instructions:

1. In a small saucepan, combine the soy sauce, mirin, honey or brown sugar, rice vinegar, minced garlic, and grated ginger. Bring the mixture to a simmer over medium heat.
2. In a small bowl, mix the cornstarch with 2 tablespoons of water to make a slurry, ensuring there are no lumps.
3. Gradually pour the cornstarch slurry into the simmering sauce, stirring constantly until the sauce thickens. Remove the sauce from the heat and let it cool to room temperature.
4. Place the thinly sliced beef in a shallow dish or resealable plastic bag. Pour half of the cooled teriyaki sauce over the beef, reserving the other half for basting.
5. Marinate the beef in the refrigerator for at least 30 minutes, or preferably up to 2 hours, to allow the flavors to meld.
6. Preheat your grill to medium-high heat. If using wooden skewers, remove them from the water and pat them dry.

7. Thread the marinated beef slices onto the skewers, folding them back and forth to create an accordion-like pattern.
8. Grill the Teriyaki Beef Skewers for 2-3 minutes per side, or until the beef is cooked to your desired level of doneness, basting with the reserved teriyaki sauce as you grill.
9. Once cooked, remove the skewers from the grill and let them rest for a few minutes.
10. Garnish the Teriyaki Beef Skewers with sesame seeds and chopped green onions, if desired.
11. Serve the skewers hot with steamed rice and your favorite vegetables for a complete meal.
12. Enjoy your delicious homemade Teriyaki Beef Skewers, packed with flavor and perfect for grilling season!

These skewers are perfect for summer cookouts, parties, or anytime you're craving a taste of Japanese-inspired cuisine.

Hawaiian Sweet Rolls

Ingredients:

- 4 cups all-purpose flour
- 1/2 cup granulated sugar
- 1 packet (2 1/4 teaspoons) active dry yeast
- 1/2 cup warm water (about 110°F/45°C)
- 1/2 cup pineapple juice
- 1/2 cup milk
- 1/2 cup unsalted butter, melted
- 2 large eggs
- 1 teaspoon salt

Instructions:

1. In a small bowl, combine the warm water and yeast. Let it sit for 5-10 minutes, or until frothy.
2. In a large mixing bowl or the bowl of a stand mixer, combine the flour, sugar, and salt.
3. In a separate bowl, whisk together the pineapple juice, milk, melted butter, and eggs.
4. Add the yeast mixture to the wet ingredients and mix well.
5. Gradually add the wet ingredients to the dry ingredients, mixing until a soft dough forms.
6. Knead the dough on a floured surface for about 5-7 minutes, or until it becomes smooth and elastic. Alternatively, you can use a stand mixer fitted with a dough hook attachment and knead the dough on medium speed for about 5 minutes.
7. Place the dough in a greased bowl, cover it with a clean kitchen towel or plastic wrap, and let it rise in a warm, draft-free place for 1-1.5 hours, or until doubled in size.
8. Once the dough has risen, punch it down to release the air bubbles.
9. Divide the dough into 12 equal pieces and shape each piece into a ball.
10. Place the dough balls in a greased 9x13-inch baking pan, leaving a little space between each roll.
11. Cover the pan with a clean kitchen towel or plastic wrap and let the rolls rise for an additional 30-45 minutes, or until they have doubled in size.
12. Preheat your oven to 350°F (175°C).

13. Bake the rolls in the preheated oven for 20-25 minutes, or until they are golden brown on top and sound hollow when tapped on the bottom.
14. Remove the rolls from the oven and let them cool in the pan for a few minutes before transferring them to a wire rack to cool completely.
15. Serve the Hawaiian Sweet Rolls warm or at room temperature, and enjoy their soft and fluffy texture!

These homemade Hawaiian Sweet Rolls are sure to be a hit with your family and friends. They're perfect for any occasion and can be enjoyed in a variety of ways.

Shoyu Chicken

Ingredients:

- 8 bone-in, skin-on chicken thighs
- 1 cup low-sodium soy sauce
- 1 cup water
- 1/2 cup brown sugar
- 1/4 cup mirin (Japanese sweet rice wine)
- 3 cloves garlic, minced
- 1-inch piece of ginger, peeled and grated
- 2 green onions, chopped (for garnish)
- Sesame seeds (for garnish, optional)

Instructions:

1. In a large mixing bowl or resealable plastic bag, combine the soy sauce, water, brown sugar, mirin, minced garlic, and grated ginger. Stir or shake well to dissolve the sugar and combine the ingredients.
2. Add the chicken thighs to the marinade, making sure they are well coated. Seal the bag or cover the bowl, and refrigerate for at least 2 hours, or preferably overnight, to allow the flavors to meld.
3. Preheat your oven to 375°F (190°C).
4. Transfer the chicken thighs and marinade to a baking dish or oven-safe skillet.
5. Bake the chicken in the preheated oven for 30-35 minutes, or until the chicken is cooked through and the internal temperature reaches 165°F (74°C). Baste the chicken with the marinade halfway through the cooking time to keep it moist and flavorful.
6. Once the chicken is cooked, remove it from the oven and let it rest for a few minutes.
7. Serve the Shoyu Chicken hot, garnished with chopped green onions and sesame seeds if desired.
8. Enjoy your delicious homemade Shoyu Chicken with steamed rice and your favorite vegetables!

Shoyu Chicken is a comforting and flavorful dish that's perfect for a weeknight dinner or for serving at gatherings and potlucks. The tender chicken and rich marinade make for a satisfying meal that's sure to be a hit with family and friends.

Lomi Lomi Salmon

Ingredients:

- 1 lb fresh salmon fillet, skin removed
- 2 ripe tomatoes, diced
- 1 small sweet onion, finely chopped
- 2 green onions, thinly sliced
- 1-2 serrano or jalapeño peppers, seeded and finely chopped (optional, for heat)
- 1 tablespoon Hawaiian salt or sea salt
- 1 tablespoon lemon or lime juice
- Freshly ground black pepper, to taste
- Fresh cilantro or parsley, chopped (for garnish, optional)

Instructions:

1. Rinse the salmon fillet under cold water and pat it dry with paper towels. Cut the salmon into small, bite-sized cubes.
2. In a large mixing bowl, combine the diced tomatoes, chopped sweet onion, sliced green onions, and chopped peppers (if using).
3. Add the salmon cubes to the bowl with the vegetables.
4. Sprinkle the Hawaiian salt or sea salt over the salmon and vegetables.
5. Squeeze the lemon or lime juice over the mixture, and add freshly ground black pepper to taste.
6. Gently toss all the ingredients together until well combined.
7. Cover the bowl with plastic wrap and refrigerate for at least 1 hour, or up to 4 hours, to allow the flavors to meld.
8. Before serving, give the Lomi Lomi Salmon a final stir. Taste and adjust the seasoning if necessary.
9. Transfer the Lomi Lomi Salmon to a serving dish and garnish with chopped cilantro or parsley if desired.
10. Serve the Lomi Lomi Salmon chilled as a refreshing side dish or appetizer.
11. Enjoy your homemade Lomi Lomi Salmon, bursting with fresh flavors and vibrant colors!

Lomi Lomi Salmon is a light and refreshing dish that's perfect for summer gatherings, picnics, or anytime you're craving a taste of Hawaiian cuisine. It pairs well with poi, rice, or as a topping for grilled fish or seafood.

Hawaiian Garlic Shrimp

Ingredients:

- 1 pound large shrimp, peeled and deveined
- 6 cloves garlic, minced
- 1/4 cup butter
- 1/4 cup olive oil
- 1/4 cup chicken broth
- 2 tablespoons lemon juice
- Salt and pepper to taste
- Chopped parsley for garnish (optional)

Instructions:

1. Prepare the Shrimp:
    - Rinse the shrimp under cold water and pat dry with paper towels.
    - Season the shrimp with salt and pepper to taste.
2. Make the Garlic Butter Sauce:
    - In a large skillet, melt the butter over medium heat.
    - Add the minced garlic to the skillet and cook until fragrant, about 1-2 minutes, stirring constantly to prevent burning.
    - Stir in the olive oil, chicken broth, and lemon juice. Cook for another 1-2 minutes, allowing the flavors to meld together.
3. Cook the Shrimp:
    - Increase the heat to medium-high and add the seasoned shrimp to the skillet.
    - Cook the shrimp for 2-3 minutes on each side, or until they turn pink and opaque.
    - Be careful not to overcook the shrimp, as they can become tough and rubbery.
4. Serve:
    - Once the shrimp are cooked through, remove the skillet from the heat.
    - Transfer the shrimp to a serving platter, pouring the garlic butter sauce over the top.
    - Garnish with chopped parsley if desired.
    - Serve hot with steamed rice or your favorite side dishes.

Enjoy your delicious Hawaiian garlic shrimp! Feel free to customize the recipe by adding additional spices or ingredients to suit your taste preferences.

Lau Lau

Ingredients:

- 1 pound pork butt, thinly sliced
- 1/2 pound salted butterfish or cod, cut into pieces
- Taro leaves (fresh or frozen, thawed)
- Sea salt
- Ti leaves or banana leaves (for wrapping, optional)

Instructions:

1. Prepare the Taro Leaves:
    - If you're using fresh taro leaves, remove the tough stems and veins from each leaf. If you're using frozen taro leaves, ensure they're thawed completely.
    - Blanch the taro leaves in boiling water for a few seconds to soften them. Remove from water and set aside.
2. Season the Pork and Fish:
    - Season the pork slices with sea salt.
    - Rinse the salted butterfish or cod under cold water to remove excess salt. Pat dry with paper towels.
3. Assemble the Lau Lau:
    - Lay a taro leaf flat on a clean surface.
    - Place a piece of pork and a piece of fish in the center of the leaf.
    - Sprinkle with a little sea salt.
    - Fold the sides of the leaf over the pork and fish, then fold the top and bottom of the leaf to encase the filling completely.
    - If desired, wrap the Lau Lau in ti leaves or banana leaves to help hold the shape and add flavor. Use kitchen twine to secure the leaves if necessary.
4. Steam the Lau Lau:
    - Arrange the Lau Lau in a steamer basket or pot.
    - Steam the Lau Lau for about 3-4 hours, or until the pork is tender and cooked through.
    - Check the water level periodically and replenish if necessary to prevent it from drying out.
5. Serve:
    - Once cooked, carefully unwrap the Lau Lau from the leaves.
    - Serve hot with steamed rice or poi, and enjoy the tender, flavorful pork and fish wrapped in taro leaves.

Lau Lau is a labor of love, so take your time when assembling and steaming them to ensure the best results. Feel free to customize the filling with your favorite meats or additional seasonings.

Mango BBQ Ribs

Ingredients:

- 2 racks of pork ribs (about 4-5 pounds total)
- 2 ripe mangoes, peeled, pitted, and diced
- 1 cup ketchup
- 1/2 cup apple cider vinegar
- 1/4 cup brown sugar
- 2 tablespoons Worcestershire sauce
- 2 tablespoons soy sauce
- 2 cloves garlic, minced
- 1 teaspoon ground ginger
- 1/2 teaspoon smoked paprika
- Salt and black pepper to taste
- Olive oil

Instructions:

1. Preheat the Oven:
    - Preheat your oven to 300°F (150°C).
2. Prepare the Ribs:
    - Rinse the ribs under cold water and pat them dry with paper towels.
    - Remove the thin membrane from the back of the ribs for better flavor penetration. Use a knife to loosen the membrane from one end of the rack, then grab it with a paper towel and peel it off.
3. Season the Ribs:
    - Rub the ribs all over with olive oil and season generously with salt and black pepper.
4. Make the Mango BBQ Sauce:
    - In a blender or food processor, combine the diced mangoes, ketchup, apple cider vinegar, brown sugar, Worcestershire sauce, soy sauce, minced garlic, ground ginger, and smoked paprika.
    - Blend until smooth. Taste and adjust seasoning if needed.
5. Cook the Ribs:
    - Place the seasoned ribs on a baking sheet lined with aluminum foil or parchment paper.
    - Brush the ribs generously with the mango BBQ sauce, reserving some sauce for later.
    - Cover the ribs tightly with aluminum foil.
6. Bake the Ribs:
    - Bake the ribs in the preheated oven for 2.5 to 3 hours, or until the meat is tender and starts to pull away from the bones.
7. Finish on the Grill (Optional):
    - Preheat your grill to medium-high heat.
    - Remove the ribs from the oven and carefully unwrap them.
    - Place the ribs on the grill and brush them with more mango BBQ sauce.

- Grill for 5-10 minutes, flipping once, until the sauce caramelizes slightly and the ribs are charred in spots.
8. Serve:
    - Once done, let the ribs rest for a few minutes before slicing them into individual portions.
    - Serve the mango BBQ ribs hot with extra sauce on the side.

Enjoy the tender, flavorful goodness of mango BBQ ribs! They're perfect for a summer barbecue or any occasion where you want to impress with delicious ribs.

Taro Chips with Pineapple Salsa

Ingredients:

For Taro Chips:

- 2 large taro roots
- Vegetable oil for frying
- Salt to taste

For Pineapple Salsa:

- 2 cups diced fresh pineapple
- 1/2 red onion, finely chopped
- 1 red bell pepper, diced
- 1 jalapeño pepper, seeded and minced (optional for heat)
- 1/4 cup chopped fresh cilantro
- Juice of 1 lime
- Salt and pepper to taste

Instructions:

For Taro Chips:

1. Prepare the Taro:
   - Peel the taro roots and slice them thinly using a mandoline slicer or a sharp knife. Make sure the slices are uniform in thickness for even frying.
2. Fry the Taro Chips:
   - Heat vegetable oil in a deep fryer or a heavy-bottomed pot to 350°F (175°C).
   - Carefully add the taro slices in batches to the hot oil, making sure not to overcrowd the pot.
   - Fry the taro slices until golden brown and crispy, about 3-4 minutes per batch.
   - Use a slotted spoon to transfer the fried taro chips to a paper towel-lined plate to drain excess oil.
   - Season the taro chips with salt while they're still warm.

For Pineapple Salsa:

1. Prepare the Pineapple Salsa:
     - In a mixing bowl, combine the diced pineapple, chopped red onion, diced red bell pepper, minced jalapeño (if using), and chopped cilantro.
     - Squeeze the lime juice over the salsa and toss gently to combine.
     - Season with salt and pepper to taste.

Assembly:

1. Serve:
     - Arrange the crispy taro chips on a serving platter.
     - Serve the pineapple salsa in a bowl alongside the taro chips.
     - Optionally, garnish the salsa with additional cilantro leaves for presentation.
2. Enjoy:
     - Dip the taro chips into the pineapple salsa and enjoy the delicious combination of flavors and textures.

These taro chips with pineapple salsa are perfect for parties, gatherings, or anytime you're craving a tropical and crunchy snack.

Pupus (Appetizer Platter)

Ingredients:

For Savory Options:

- Sushi rolls or sushi-grade fish slices
- Edamame (steamed soybeans)
- Ahi poke (Hawaiian marinated raw tuna)
- Kalua pork sliders (shredded pork on small rolls)
- Teriyaki chicken skewers
- Coconut shrimp with sweet chili sauce
- Spam musubi (sliced Spam on a block of rice, wrapped in nori)
- Crab Rangoon (crispy wontons filled with cream cheese and crab meat)
- Vegetable spring rolls with dipping sauce
- Mini meatballs glazed with teriyaki sauce

For Fresh and Light Options:

- Fresh fruit skewers (pineapple, melon, grapes)
- Caprese skewers (mozzarella balls, cherry tomatoes, and basil leaves)
- Cucumber avocado rolls (thinly sliced cucumber wrapped around avocado)
- Seaweed salad
- Hawaiian-style ceviche with fresh fish, lime juice, onions, and peppers
- Veggie crudité with hummus or ranch dip

For Dipping and Spreads:

- Sweet chili sauce
- Teriyaki sauce
- Soy sauce with wasabi and pickled ginger
- Sriracha mayo
- Ponzu sauce
- Peanut sauce
- Guacamole
- Tzatziki

Assembly:

1. Prepare Ingredients:
   - Cook and prepare all the items according to their respective recipes. Keep warm items warm and cold items chilled until ready to assemble.
2. Arrange on Platter:
   - Choose a large platter or board to arrange your pupus.
   - Start by placing larger items like sushi rolls and sliders around the edges of the platter.
   - Fill the gaps with smaller items like skewers, sushi-grade fish slices, and bite-sized appetizers.
   - Use small bowls or ramekins for dips and sauces, placing them strategically throughout the platter.
3. Garnish and Decorate:
   - Garnish the platter with fresh herbs, sliced fruits, or edible flowers for an attractive presentation.
   - Use small serving utensils or toothpicks for guests to pick up the items easily.
4. Serve and Enjoy:
   - Place the pupus platter in the center of your serving area and invite guests to help themselves.
   - Enjoy the delicious variety of flavors and textures with friends and family!

Creating a pupus platter allows for customization based on your preferences and the preferences of your guests. Feel free to mix and match items and adjust quantities according to the size of your gathering.

Coconut Shrimp

Ingredients:

- 1 pound large shrimp, peeled and deveined
- 1 cup sweetened shredded coconut
- 1 cup panko breadcrumbs
- 1/2 cup all-purpose flour
- 2 large eggs
- 1 teaspoon garlic powder
- 1/2 teaspoon paprika
- 1/2 teaspoon salt
- 1/4 teaspoon black pepper
- Vegetable oil, for frying
- Sweet chili sauce, for dipping (optional)

Instructions:

1. Prepare the Shrimp:
    - Rinse the shrimp under cold water and pat them dry with paper towels.
    - In a small bowl, mix together the garlic powder, paprika, salt, and black pepper.
    - Season the shrimp with the spice mixture, ensuring they are evenly coated.
2. Prepare the Coating Station:
    - Set up three shallow bowls. In the first bowl, place the all-purpose flour. In the second bowl, beat the eggs. In the third bowl, combine the sweetened shredded coconut and panko breadcrumbs.
3. Coat the Shrimp:
    - Working with one shrimp at a time, dredge it in the flour, shaking off any excess.
    - Dip the shrimp into the beaten eggs, allowing any excess to drip off.
    - Coat the shrimp generously with the coconut-panko mixture, pressing gently to adhere. Repeat with the remaining shrimp.
4. Fry the Shrimp:
    - In a large skillet or deep fryer, heat vegetable oil to 350°F (175°C).
    - Carefully add the coated shrimp to the hot oil in batches, making sure not to overcrowd the skillet.
    - Fry the shrimp for 2-3 minutes on each side, or until they are golden brown and crispy.

- Use a slotted spoon to transfer the cooked shrimp to a plate lined with paper towels to drain excess oil.
5. Serve:
    - Serve the coconut shrimp hot with sweet chili sauce for dipping, if desired.
    - Garnish with chopped cilantro or a squeeze of lime juice for extra flavor.

Enjoy the crispy, golden coconut shrimp as a delicious appetizer or main dish. They're sure to be a hit at any gathering!

Malasadas (Portuguese Doughnuts)

Ingredients:

- 4 cups all-purpose flour
- 1/2 cup granulated sugar
- 1 teaspoon salt
- 1 packet (2 1/4 teaspoons) active dry yeast
- 3/4 cup warm water (110°F/45°C)
- 4 large eggs
- 1/4 cup unsalted butter, softened
- 1/2 cup evaporated milk
- 1 teaspoon vanilla extract
- Vegetable oil, for frying
- Granulated sugar, for coating

Instructions:

1. Activate the Yeast:
   - In a small bowl, dissolve the yeast in warm water. Let it sit for about 5 minutes until foamy.
2. Make the Dough:
   - In a large mixing bowl, combine the flour, sugar, and salt.
   - Add the activated yeast mixture, eggs, softened butter, evaporated milk, and vanilla extract to the dry ingredients.
   - Mix everything together until a smooth dough forms. If the dough is too sticky, add a little more flour, 1 tablespoon at a time.
3. Knead the Dough:
   - Transfer the dough to a floured surface and knead it for about 5-7 minutes until it becomes smooth and elastic.
4. Proof the Dough:
   - Place the dough in a greased bowl, cover it with plastic wrap or a clean kitchen towel, and let it rise in a warm place for about 1 to 1 1/2 hours, or until doubled in size.
5. Shape the Doughnuts:
   - After the dough has risen, punch it down and divide it into small balls, about 2 inches in diameter.
   - Place the dough balls on a lightly floured baking sheet, cover them, and let them rise again for about 30-45 minutes.
6. Fry the Malasadas:

- In a large, deep skillet or Dutch oven, heat vegetable oil to 350°F (175°C).
- Carefully add a few doughnuts to the hot oil, making sure not to overcrowd the pan.
- Fry the doughnuts for about 2-3 minutes on each side, or until they are golden brown and cooked through.
- Use a slotted spoon to transfer the fried malasadas to a plate lined with paper towels to drain excess oil.

7. Coat with Sugar:
   - While the malasadas are still warm, roll them in granulated sugar until they are evenly coated.
8. Serve and Enjoy:
   - Serve the malasadas warm and enjoy them as a delicious treat!

These homemade malasadas are best enjoyed fresh and warm. They're perfect for breakfast, dessert, or any time you're craving a sweet indulgence!

Huli Huli Tofu Skewers

Ingredients:

For the Tofu:

- 1 block firm tofu, pressed and drained
- 1/4 cup soy sauce
- 1/4 cup pineapple juice
- 2 tablespoons brown sugar
- 2 cloves garlic, minced
- 1 teaspoon grated ginger
- 1 tablespoon sesame oil
- 1 tablespoon rice vinegar
- Salt and pepper to taste

For the Skewers:

- Wooden or metal skewers
- Bell peppers, onions, cherry tomatoes, or any other vegetables of your choice, cut into chunks

For Garnish (optional):

- Sesame seeds
- Chopped green onions
- Pineapple chunks

Instructions:

1. Prepare the Tofu:
    - Cut the pressed and drained tofu into cubes or rectangles, depending on your preference.
2. Make the Marinade:
    - In a bowl, whisk together the soy sauce, pineapple juice, brown sugar, minced garlic, grated ginger, sesame oil, rice vinegar, salt, and pepper.
3. Marinate the Tofu:
    - Place the tofu cubes in a shallow dish or resealable plastic bag.

- Pour the marinade over the tofu, making sure it's evenly coated. Marinate for at least 30 minutes, or overnight in the refrigerator for best flavor.
4. Prepare the Skewers:
    - If you're using wooden skewers, soak them in water for at least 30 minutes to prevent them from burning on the grill.
    - Thread the marinated tofu cubes and vegetables onto the skewers, alternating between tofu and vegetables.
5. Grill the Skewers:
    - Preheat your grill to medium-high heat.
    - Lightly oil the grill grates to prevent sticking.
    - Place the tofu skewers on the grill and cook for about 5-7 minutes on each side, or until the tofu is lightly charred and the vegetables are tender.
6. Baste with Marinade:
    - While grilling, brush the tofu skewers with any remaining marinade to enhance the flavor.
7. Serve:
    - Once cooked through, remove the tofu skewers from the grill and transfer them to a serving platter.
    - Garnish with sesame seeds, chopped green onions, and pineapple chunks if desired.
    - Serve hot and enjoy these delicious Huli Huli tofu skewers!

These skewers are perfect for a vegetarian barbecue or as a flavorful addition to any meal. They're packed with Hawaiian-inspired flavors and are sure to be a hit with everyone!

Mochiko Chicken

Ingredients:

- 2 pounds boneless, skinless chicken thighs or breasts, cut into bite-sized pieces
- 1 cup mochiko (sweet rice flour)
- 1/4 cup cornstarch
- 1/4 cup soy sauce
- 1/4 cup granulated sugar
- 2 cloves garlic, minced
- 1 tablespoon grated ginger
- 1 tablespoon sesame oil
- 2 green onions, finely chopped (optional)
- Vegetable oil, for frying
- Sesame seeds and sliced green onions, for garnish (optional)

Instructions:

1. Prepare the Chicken:
    - Cut the chicken thighs or breasts into bite-sized pieces and place them in a large mixing bowl.
2. Make the Marinade:
    - In a separate bowl, combine the mochiko, cornstarch, soy sauce, sugar, minced garlic, grated ginger, sesame oil, and chopped green onions (if using). Mix until well combined and smooth.
3. Marinate the Chicken:
    - Pour the marinade over the chicken pieces and toss until they are evenly coated. Cover the bowl with plastic wrap and refrigerate for at least 2 hours, or overnight for best flavor.
4. Fry the Chicken:
    - In a large skillet or deep fryer, heat vegetable oil to 350°F (175°C).
    - Remove the marinated chicken from the refrigerator and give it a quick stir to ensure the pieces are evenly coated.
    - Carefully add the chicken to the hot oil in batches, making sure not to overcrowd the pan.
    - Fry the chicken for about 6-8 minutes, or until golden brown and cooked through. You may need to flip the chicken pieces halfway through cooking for even browning.
5. Drain and Garnish:

- Use a slotted spoon to transfer the cooked chicken to a plate lined with paper towels to drain excess oil.
- Garnish the mochiko chicken with sesame seeds and sliced green onions, if desired.

6. Serve:
    - Serve the mochiko chicken hot as a delicious appetizer or main dish. It pairs well with steamed rice and a side of vegetables.

Enjoy the crispy and flavorful goodness of homemade mochiko chicken! It's a beloved Hawaiian dish that's sure to be a hit with family and friends.

Pineapple Upside-Down Cake

Ingredients:

For the Pineapple Topping:

- 1/4 cup unsalted butter
- 1/2 cup packed brown sugar
- 1 can (20 ounces) pineapple slices in juice, drained
- Maraschino cherries (optional)

For the Cake Batter:

- 1 1/2 cups all-purpose flour
- 3/4 cup granulated sugar
- 2 teaspoons baking powder
- 1/4 teaspoon salt
- 1/2 cup unsalted butter, softened
- 2 large eggs
- 1 teaspoon vanilla extract
- 1/2 cup pineapple juice (reserved from canned pineapple)
- 1/4 cup milk

Instructions:

1. Preheat the Oven:
    - Preheat your oven to 350°F (175°C). Grease a 9-inch round cake pan or a 9x9-inch square cake pan.
2. Prepare the Pineapple Topping:
    - In a small saucepan, melt the 1/4 cup of butter over medium heat.
    - Stir in the brown sugar until dissolved and bubbling.
    - Pour the butter-sugar mixture into the bottom of the greased cake pan, spreading it evenly.
    - Arrange the pineapple slices on top of the sugar mixture in a single layer. You can place a maraschino cherry in the center of each pineapple slice if desired.
3. Make the Cake Batter:
    - In a medium bowl, whisk together the flour, sugar, baking powder, and salt.
    - In a separate large bowl, beat the softened butter until creamy.

- Add the eggs, one at a time, beating well after each addition. Stir in the vanilla extract.
- Gradually add the dry flour mixture to the butter mixture, alternating with the pineapple juice and milk, until well combined. Mix until smooth.

4. Assemble and Bake:
   - Pour the cake batter over the pineapple slices in the cake pan, spreading it evenly to cover the fruit.
   - Tap the pan gently on the counter to remove any air bubbles.
   - Bake in the preheated oven for 35-40 minutes, or until a toothpick inserted into the center of the cake comes out clean.
5. Cool and Invert:
   - Remove the cake from the oven and let it cool in the pan for 5-10 minutes.
   - Carefully run a knife around the edges of the cake to loosen it from the pan.
   - Place a serving plate or cake stand upside down on top of the cake pan, then quickly and carefully invert the cake onto the plate. Be cautious, as the pan and syrup will be hot.
6. Serve:
   - Serve the pineapple upside-down cake warm or at room temperature.
   - Optionally, garnish with additional maraschino cherries or whipped cream.

Enjoy the nostalgic and delicious flavor of homemade pineapple upside-down cake! It's a perfect dessert for any occasion.

Hawaiian Plate Lunch

Ingredients:

For the Main Dish (Choose One or More):

- Kalua pork: shredded, slow-cooked pork flavored with Hawaiian sea salt and traditionally cooked in an underground oven called an imu.
- Teriyaki chicken: grilled or pan-fried chicken marinated in a sweet and savory teriyaki sauce.
- Loco moco: a Hawaiian comfort food dish consisting of a hamburger patty served on rice, topped with a fried egg and smothered in gravy.
- Chicken katsu: breaded and fried chicken cutlets served with a tangy tonkatsu sauce.
- Lau Lau: pork, fish, or chicken wrapped in taro leaves and steamed until tender.

For the Rice:

- White rice or sticky rice (2 scoops per plate)

For the Macaroni Salad:

- 2 cups cooked elbow macaroni
- 1/2 cup mayonnaise
- 2 tablespoons apple cider vinegar
- 1 tablespoon granulated sugar
- 1 carrot, grated
- 1/4 cup finely chopped celery
- Salt and pepper to taste

Instructions:

1. Prepare the Main Dish:
   - Choose one or more of the main dishes listed above and prepare them according to their respective recipes. Keep them warm until ready to serve.
2. Cook the Rice:
   - Cook the white rice or sticky rice according to the package instructions. Keep warm until ready to serve.
3. Make the Macaroni Salad:

- In a large mixing bowl, combine the cooked elbow macaroni, mayonnaise, apple cider vinegar, sugar, grated carrot, and chopped celery.
- Season with salt and pepper to taste and mix until well combined. Adjust the seasoning if necessary.

4. Assemble the Plate Lunch:
    - On each plate, place two scoops of cooked rice.
    - Add a generous portion of the main dish(es) of your choice next to the rice.
    - Scoop a serving of macaroni salad onto the plate, typically on the side of the rice and main dish.
5. Serve:
    - Serve the Hawaiian plate lunch hot and enjoy the delicious combination of flavors and textures!

Hawaiian plate lunch is a hearty and satisfying meal that captures the essence of Hawaiian cuisine. It's perfect for lunch or dinner, and it's a great way to experience the diverse flavors of Hawaii.

Banana Macadamia Nut Bread

Ingredients:

- 2 cups all-purpose flour
- 1 teaspoon baking soda
- 1/4 teaspoon salt
- 1/2 cup unsalted butter, melted
- 3/4 cup granulated sugar
- 2 large eggs
- 1 teaspoon vanilla extract
- 3 ripe bananas, mashed
- 1/2 cup chopped macadamia nuts
- Optional: additional chopped macadamia nuts for topping

Instructions:

1. Preheat the Oven:
    - Preheat your oven to 350°F (175°C). Grease a 9x5-inch loaf pan or line it with parchment paper.
2. Prepare the Dry Ingredients:
    - In a medium bowl, whisk together the all-purpose flour, baking soda, and salt until well combined. Set aside.
3. Mix the Wet Ingredients:
    - In a large mixing bowl, mix together the melted butter and granulated sugar until smooth.
    - Add the eggs, one at a time, mixing well after each addition.
    - Stir in the vanilla extract and mashed bananas until combined.
4. Combine Wet and Dry Ingredients:
    - Gradually add the dry ingredients to the wet ingredients, stirring until just combined. Be careful not to overmix.
    - Fold in the chopped macadamia nuts until evenly distributed throughout the batter.
5. Bake the Bread:
    - Pour the batter into the prepared loaf pan, spreading it out evenly.
    - If desired, sprinkle additional chopped macadamia nuts on top of the batter for added texture and visual appeal.
    - Bake in the preheated oven for 50-60 minutes, or until a toothpick inserted into the center of the bread comes out clean.
6. Cool and Serve:

- Once baked, remove the banana macadamia nut bread from the oven and let it cool in the pan for 10-15 minutes.
- Carefully transfer the bread to a wire rack to cool completely before slicing.
- Slice and serve the bread warm or at room temperature. Enjoy!

This banana macadamia nut bread is moist, flavorful, and perfect for breakfast, brunch, or as a snack any time of the day. The combination of ripe bananas and crunchy macadamia nuts creates a wonderful texture and flavor experience that you'll love.

Ahi Tuna Tacos

Ingredients:

For the Ahi Tuna:

- 1 pound sushi-grade ahi tuna, cut into small cubes or thin slices
- 2 tablespoons soy sauce
- 1 tablespoon sesame oil
- 1 teaspoon grated ginger
- 1 teaspoon minced garlic
- 1 tablespoon lime juice
- Salt and pepper to taste
- Vegetable oil for searing

For the Tacos:

- 8 small corn or flour tortillas, warmed
- 1 cup shredded cabbage or lettuce
- 1/2 cup diced mango or pineapple
- 1/4 cup diced red onion
- 1/4 cup chopped cilantro
- Sliced jalapeños (optional, for heat)
- Lime wedges, for serving

For the Sauce:

- 1/4 cup mayonnaise
- 2 tablespoons sriracha sauce (adjust to taste)
- 1 tablespoon lime juice
- Salt and pepper to taste

Instructions:

1. Marinate the Ahi Tuna:
   - In a bowl, whisk together the soy sauce, sesame oil, grated ginger, minced garlic, lime juice, salt, and pepper.
   - Add the cubed or sliced ahi tuna to the marinade and toss to coat. Let it marinate in the refrigerator for at least 15-20 minutes.
2. Prepare the Sauce:

- In a small bowl, mix together the mayonnaise, sriracha sauce, lime juice, salt, and pepper to make the spicy mayo sauce. Adjust the sriracha sauce to your desired level of spiciness. Set aside.

3. Cook the Ahi Tuna:
   - Heat a small amount of vegetable oil in a skillet or grill pan over high heat.
   - Once the oil is hot, add the marinated ahi tuna cubes or slices to the skillet in a single layer, making sure not to overcrowd the pan.
   - Sear the tuna for about 1-2 minutes on each side, or until browned on the outside and still pink in the center. Be careful not to overcook the tuna.
   - Remove the tuna from the skillet and set it aside.
4. Assemble the Tacos:
   - Warm the tortillas in a dry skillet or microwave until soft and pliable.
   - Place a spoonful of shredded cabbage or lettuce on each tortilla.
   - Top with the seared ahi tuna, diced mango or pineapple, diced red onion, chopped cilantro, and sliced jalapeños if using.
   - Drizzle the spicy mayo sauce over the tacos.
5. Serve:
   - Serve the ahi tuna tacos immediately, garnished with lime wedges on the side for squeezing.

Enjoy these flavorful and refreshing ahi tuna tacos as a delicious appetizer or main dish. They're perfect for a seafood-themed meal or for any occasion when you're craving something light and satisfying!

Hawaiian Pizza

Ingredients:

For the Pizza Dough:

- 1 pound pizza dough (store-bought or homemade)

For the Pizza Toppings:

- 1/2 cup pizza sauce or marinara sauce
- 2 cups shredded mozzarella cheese
- 1 cup diced ham or Canadian bacon
- 1 cup pineapple chunks (fresh or canned, drained)
- Red pepper flakes (optional, for added heat)
- Fresh basil leaves (optional, for garnish)

Instructions:

1. Preheat the Oven:
    - Preheat your oven to the highest temperature setting (usually around 475-500°F or 245-260°C). If you have a pizza stone, place it in the oven to preheat as well.
2. Prepare the Dough:
    - On a lightly floured surface, roll out the pizza dough into a circle or rectangle, depending on your preference and the shape of your pizza pan.
3. Assemble the Pizza:
    - Transfer the rolled-out pizza dough to a lightly greased pizza pan or baking sheet.
    - Spread the pizza sauce evenly over the dough, leaving a small border around the edges.
    - Sprinkle the shredded mozzarella cheese over the sauce.
    - Arrange the diced ham or Canadian bacon and pineapple chunks evenly on top of the cheese.
    - If desired, sprinkle red pepper flakes over the toppings for added heat.
4. Bake the Pizza:
    - Carefully transfer the assembled pizza to the preheated oven, either directly onto the pizza stone or onto the middle rack of the oven.

- Bake for 10-15 minutes, or until the crust is golden brown and the cheese is bubbly and melted.
5. Serve:
    - Once baked, remove the Hawaiian pizza from the oven and let it cool slightly.
    - Garnish with fresh basil leaves if desired.
    - Slice and serve the pizza hot, and enjoy!

Hawaiian pizza is a crowd-pleaser with its combination of sweet pineapple, savory ham, and gooey melted cheese. Feel free to customize the toppings according to your preferences, and enjoy this delicious homemade pizza with family and friends!

Loco Moco Burger

Ingredients:

For the Burger Patties:

- 1 1/2 pounds ground beef (or ground turkey, chicken, or plant-based alternative)
- Salt and pepper to taste
- 1 tablespoon Worcestershire sauce
- 1 tablespoon soy sauce
- 1 teaspoon garlic powder
- 1 teaspoon onion powder

For the Gravy:

- 2 tablespoons unsalted butter
- 2 tablespoons all-purpose flour
- 1 1/2 cups beef or chicken broth
- 1 tablespoon soy sauce
- Salt and pepper to taste

For Assembling the Burger:

- Burger buns
- Cooked white rice
- Fried eggs (1 per burger)
- Sliced scallions or chopped parsley for garnish (optional)

Instructions:

1. Prepare the Burger Patties:
    - In a large mixing bowl, combine the ground beef with salt, pepper, Worcestershire sauce, soy sauce, garlic powder, and onion powder. Mix until well combined.
    - Divide the seasoned meat mixture into equal portions and shape them into burger patties.
2. Cook the Burger Patties:
    - Heat a grill or skillet over medium-high heat.

- Cook the burger patties for about 4-5 minutes on each side, or until they reach your desired level of doneness. Make sure to cook them thoroughly if using ground beef.
3. Make the Gravy:
    - In a small saucepan, melt the butter over medium heat.
    - Whisk in the all-purpose flour to form a roux. Cook for 1-2 minutes, stirring constantly.
    - Gradually whisk in the beef or chicken broth until smooth.
    - Stir in the soy sauce and season with salt and pepper to taste.
    - Cook the gravy for a few minutes until it thickens to your desired consistency. Remove from heat and set aside.
4. Assemble the Loco Moco Burger:
    - Toast the burger buns if desired.
    - Place a cooked burger patty on the bottom half of each burger bun.
    - Top each burger patty with a scoop of cooked white rice.
    - Carefully place a fried egg on top of the rice.
    - Spoon a generous amount of gravy over the fried egg.
    - Sprinkle sliced scallions or chopped parsley on top for garnish, if desired.
5. Serve:
    - Place the top half of the burger bun on each assembled Loco Moco burger.
    - Serve immediately and enjoy this delicious fusion dish!

The Loco Moco burger combines the best of both worlds – the savory goodness of a burger with the comforting flavors of Loco Moco. It's sure to be a hit at any mealtime!

Coconut Shrimp Tacos

Ingredients:

For the Coconut Shrimp:

- 1 pound large shrimp, peeled and deveined
- 1 cup sweetened shredded coconut
- 1 cup panko breadcrumbs
- 1/2 cup all-purpose flour
- 2 large eggs
- Salt and pepper to taste
- Vegetable oil for frying

For the Slaw:

- 2 cups shredded cabbage or coleslaw mix
- 1/4 cup chopped cilantro
- 2 tablespoons lime juice
- 1 tablespoon honey or maple syrup
- Salt and pepper to taste

For the Sauce:

- 1/2 cup mayonnaise
- 2 tablespoons sriracha sauce (adjust to taste)
- 1 tablespoon lime juice
- Salt and pepper to taste

For Assembling the Tacos:

- 8 small corn or flour tortillas, warmed
- Sliced avocado
- Sliced jalapeños (optional)
- Lime wedges for serving
- Additional cilantro for garnish

Instructions:

1. Prepare the Coconut Shrimp:
   - In a shallow bowl, combine the sweetened shredded coconut and panko breadcrumbs.
   - Place the all-purpose flour in another shallow bowl.
   - In a third shallow bowl, beat the eggs.
   - Season the shrimp with salt and pepper.
   - Dredge each shrimp in the flour, then dip it into the beaten eggs, and finally coat it with the coconut breadcrumb mixture, pressing gently to adhere.
   - Place the coated shrimp on a plate and refrigerate for 15-20 minutes to help set the coating.
2. Make the Slaw:
   - In a large bowl, combine the shredded cabbage or coleslaw mix with chopped cilantro, lime juice, honey or maple syrup, salt, and pepper. Toss until well combined. Set aside.
3. Prepare the Sauce:
   - In a small bowl, mix together the mayonnaise, sriracha sauce, lime juice, salt, and pepper to make the spicy mayo sauce. Adjust the sriracha sauce to your desired level of spiciness. Set aside.
4. Fry the Shrimp:
   - Heat vegetable oil in a large skillet or deep fryer to 350°F (175°C).
   - Carefully add the coated shrimp to the hot oil in batches, making sure not to overcrowd the skillet.
   - Fry the shrimp for about 2-3 minutes on each side, or until they are golden brown and cooked through.
   - Use a slotted spoon to transfer the cooked shrimp to a plate lined with paper towels to drain excess oil.
5. Assemble the Tacos:
   - Place a spoonful of the slaw on each warmed tortilla.
   - Top with a few pieces of crispy coconut shrimp.
   - Drizzle with the spicy mayo sauce.
   - Add slices of avocado and jalapeños if desired.
   - Garnish with additional cilantro and serve with lime wedges on the side.
6. Serve:
   - Serve the coconut shrimp tacos immediately, and enjoy the delicious combination of flavors and textures!

These coconut shrimp tacos are perfect for a tropical-inspired meal and are sure to be a hit with family and friends. Enjoy!

Hawaiian BBQ Meatballs

Ingredients:

For the Meatballs:

- 1 pound ground beef or pork
- 1/2 cup breadcrumbs
- 1/4 cup milk
- 1/4 cup minced onion
- 1 clove garlic, minced
- 1 large egg
- 1/2 teaspoon salt
- 1/4 teaspoon black pepper

For the Hawaiian BBQ Sauce:

- 1 cup barbecue sauce (use your favorite brand)
- 1/4 cup pineapple juice
- 2 tablespoons soy sauce
- 2 tablespoons brown sugar
- 1 tablespoon rice vinegar
- 1 teaspoon minced garlic
- 1/2 teaspoon grated ginger
- 1/4 teaspoon onion powder
- 1/4 teaspoon chili flakes (optional, for heat)
- 1 tablespoon cornstarch mixed with 1 tablespoon water (optional, for thickening)

For Garnish (optional):

- Sliced green onions
- Toasted sesame seeds

Instructions:

1. Preheat the Oven:
    - Preheat your oven to 400°F (200°C). Line a baking sheet with parchment paper or lightly grease it.
2. Make the Meatballs:

- In a large mixing bowl, combine the ground beef or pork with breadcrumbs, milk, minced onion, minced garlic, egg, salt, and black pepper. Mix until well combined.
- Shape the mixture into meatballs, about 1 inch in diameter, and place them on the prepared baking sheet.

3. Bake the Meatballs:
    - Bake the meatballs in the preheated oven for 15-20 minutes, or until they are cooked through and browned on the outside. Remove from the oven and set aside.
4. Prepare the Hawaiian BBQ Sauce:
    - In a small saucepan, combine barbecue sauce, pineapple juice, soy sauce, brown sugar, rice vinegar, minced garlic, grated ginger, onion powder, and chili flakes if using.
    - Bring the sauce to a simmer over medium heat, stirring occasionally. Let it simmer for 5-7 minutes until slightly thickened.
    - If you prefer a thicker sauce, mix the cornstarch with water to create a slurry and add it to the sauce. Cook for an additional 1-2 minutes until thickened.
5. Coat the Meatballs:
    - Place the baked meatballs in a large bowl.
    - Pour the Hawaiian BBQ sauce over the meatballs and toss gently to coat them evenly with the sauce.
6. Finish and Serve:
    - Transfer the coated meatballs to a serving dish.
    - Garnish with sliced green onions and toasted sesame seeds if desired.
    - Serve the Hawaiian BBQ meatballs as an appetizer with toothpicks or as a main dish with rice or noodles.

Enjoy the sweet and tangy flavor of these Hawaiian BBQ meatballs! They're perfect for parties, potlucks, or as a tasty weeknight meal.

Pineapple Coconut Smoothie Bowl

Ingredients:

For the Smoothie Bowl:

- 1 cup frozen pineapple chunks
- 1 ripe banana, sliced and frozen
- 1/2 cup coconut milk (or almond milk, yogurt, or coconut water)
- 1/4 cup shredded coconut
- 1 tablespoon honey or maple syrup (optional, for added sweetness)
- Juice of 1/2 lime (optional, for a tangy flavor)

For Toppings:

- Sliced fresh pineapple
- Toasted coconut flakes
- Granola
- Sliced banana
- Chia seeds
- Sliced almonds or other nuts
- Fresh berries (such as strawberries or blueberries)
- Mint leaves for garnish

Instructions:

1. Prepare the Smoothie Base:
    - In a blender, combine the frozen pineapple chunks, frozen banana slices, coconut milk, shredded coconut, honey or maple syrup (if using), and lime juice (if using).
    - Blend until smooth and creamy. If the mixture is too thick, you can add a splash of additional coconut milk to reach your desired consistency.
2. Assemble the Smoothie Bowl:
    - Pour the smoothie into a bowl.
    - Arrange your desired toppings on top of the smoothie base. You can get creative with the arrangement or simply sprinkle them over the top.
3. Add Toppings:

- Arrange sliced fresh pineapple, toasted coconut flakes, granola, sliced banana, chia seeds, sliced almonds or other nuts, and fresh berries on top of the smoothie bowl.
- Garnish with mint leaves for a fresh touch.
4. Serve:
    - Serve the pineapple coconut smoothie bowl immediately and enjoy it with a spoon!

This pineapple coconut smoothie bowl is not only delicious but also packed with vitamins, minerals, and antioxidants. It's a perfect way to start your day or refuel after a workout. Feel free to customize the toppings according to your preferences and enjoy this tropical treat!

Hawaiian Style BBQ Pulled Pork Sliders

Ingredients:

For the Pulled Pork:

- 3-4 pounds pork shoulder or pork butt, trimmed of excess fat
- 1 onion, sliced
- 4 cloves garlic, minced
- 1 cup pineapple juice
- 1/2 cup low-sodium soy sauce
- 1/4 cup ketchup
- 1/4 cup brown sugar
- 2 tablespoons rice vinegar
- 1 tablespoon grated ginger
- 1 teaspoon garlic powder
- 1 teaspoon onion powder
- 1 teaspoon ground black pepper
- Hawaiian or sea salt, to taste
- Slider buns, for serving

For Toppings (optional):

- Pineapple slices
- Coleslaw
- Sliced red onions
- Pickles
- Sriracha mayo or barbecue sauce

Instructions:

1. Prepare the Pork:
    - Place the sliced onions and minced garlic in the bottom of a slow cooker.
    - Season the pork shoulder with salt and pepper, then place it on top of the onions and garlic.
2. Make the BBQ Sauce:
    - In a mixing bowl, whisk together the pineapple juice, soy sauce, ketchup, brown sugar, rice vinegar, grated ginger, garlic powder, onion powder, and black pepper to make the BBQ sauce.
3. Cook the Pork:

- Pour the BBQ sauce over the pork shoulder in the slow cooker, making sure it's evenly coated.
- Cover and cook on low for 8-10 hours or on high for 4-6 hours, until the pork is tender and easily shreds with a fork.

4. Shred the Pork:
   - Once the pork is cooked, remove it from the slow cooker and place it on a cutting board.
   - Use two forks to shred the pork into bite-sized pieces. Discard any excess fat.
5. Assemble the Sliders:
   - Place the shredded pork back into the slow cooker with the remaining sauce, stirring to coat the pork evenly.
   - To assemble the sliders, spoon a generous amount of pulled pork onto each slider bun.
   - Top with your choice of toppings such as pineapple slices, coleslaw, sliced red onions, pickles, and a drizzle of sriracha mayo or barbecue sauce.
6. Serve:
   - Serve the Hawaiian-style BBQ pulled pork sliders immediately and enjoy!

These sliders are perfect for parties, potlucks, or game day gatherings. They're packed with flavor and are sure to be a hit with everyone!

Huli Huli Tempeh Bowl

Ingredients:

For the Huli Huli Tempeh:

- 1 package (8 ounces) tempeh, sliced into thin strips
- 1/4 cup soy sauce or tamari
- 1/4 cup pineapple juice
- 2 tablespoons brown sugar or honey
- 2 tablespoons ketchup
- 1 tablespoon rice vinegar
- 1 tablespoon sesame oil
- 2 cloves garlic, minced
- 1 teaspoon grated ginger
- 1/4 teaspoon black pepper
- Vegetable oil for grilling

For the Bowl:

- Cooked rice (white or brown)
- Sliced vegetables (such as bell peppers, carrots, cabbage, or broccoli)
- Sliced avocado
- Sliced green onions
- Sesame seeds for garnish
- Lime wedges for serving

Instructions:

1. Marinate the Tempeh:
    - In a shallow dish or bowl, whisk together the soy sauce, pineapple juice, brown sugar or honey, ketchup, rice vinegar, sesame oil, minced garlic, grated ginger, and black pepper to make the marinade.
    - Add the sliced tempeh to the marinade, making sure it is well coated. Cover and refrigerate for at least 30 minutes to allow the flavors to develop.
2. Grill the Tempeh:
    - Heat a grill pan or skillet over medium-high heat and lightly grease with vegetable oil.

- Remove the marinated tempeh from the refrigerator and place it in the hot skillet in a single layer.
- Cook for 3-4 minutes on each side, or until the tempeh is browned and caramelized, and heated through.
3. Prepare the Bowl:
    - Divide cooked rice among serving bowls.
    - Top each bowl with grilled tempeh slices and sliced vegetables of your choice.
    - Add sliced avocado and green onions on top.
4. Make the Huli Huli Sauce:
    - If desired, you can drizzle the bowls with additional Huli Huli sauce for extra flavor. You can use the remaining marinade, or prepare a fresh batch by whisking together equal parts soy sauce, pineapple juice, ketchup, and brown sugar.
5. Garnish and Serve:
    - Garnish the bowls with sesame seeds for added texture and flavor.
    - Serve the Huli Huli tempeh bowls with lime wedges on the side for squeezing.

Enjoy these delicious and nutritious Huli Huli tempeh bowls, packed with tropical flavors and wholesome ingredients! They make a satisfying meal for lunch or dinner.

Grilled Pineapple with Honey Lime Glaze

Ingredients:

- 1 ripe pineapple, peeled, cored, and cut into slices or wedges
- 1/4 cup honey
- 2 tablespoons lime juice
- Zest of 1 lime
- Pinch of salt
- Vegetable oil or cooking spray for grilling
- Optional: Fresh mint leaves for garnish

Instructions:

1. Prepare the Pineapple:
    - Preheat your grill to medium-high heat.
    - Slice the pineapple into desired shapes, such as rings or wedges, removing the tough core.
2. Make the Honey Lime Glaze:
    - In a small bowl, whisk together the honey, lime juice, lime zest, and a pinch of salt until well combined. This will be your glaze for the grilled pineapple.
3. Grill the Pineapple:
    - Lightly brush the pineapple slices or wedges with vegetable oil or spray them with cooking spray to prevent sticking.
    - Place the pineapple pieces directly onto the preheated grill grates.
    - Grill for about 2-3 minutes on each side, or until grill marks form and the pineapple is slightly caramelized.
4. Glaze the Pineapple:
    - Brush the grilled pineapple with the honey lime glaze, coating each piece evenly.
    - Continue grilling for an additional 1-2 minutes on each side, allowing the glaze to caramelize slightly.
5. Serve:
    - Remove the grilled pineapple from the grill and transfer it to a serving platter.
    - Optionally, garnish with fresh mint leaves for a pop of color and added freshness.
    - Serve the grilled pineapple warm as a delicious dessert or side dish.

Enjoy the sweet and tangy flavor of the grilled pineapple with honey lime glaze! It's a simple yet elegant dish that is sure to impress your guests and satisfy your taste buds.

Huli Huli Veggie Skewers

Ingredients:

For the Veggie Skewers:

- Assorted vegetables, such as bell peppers, onions, zucchini, mushrooms, cherry tomatoes, and pineapple, cut into bite-sized pieces
- Wooden skewers, soaked in water for at least 30 minutes to prevent burning

For the Huli Huli Marinade:

- 1/4 cup soy sauce or tamari
- 1/4 cup pineapple juice
- 2 tablespoons brown sugar or honey
- 2 tablespoons ketchup
- 1 tablespoon rice vinegar
- 1 tablespoon sesame oil
- 1 clove garlic, minced
- 1 teaspoon grated ginger
- 1/4 teaspoon black pepper

Optional Garnish:

- Chopped green onions
- Sesame seeds

Instructions:

1. Prepare the Huli Huli Marinade:
    - In a small bowl, whisk together the soy sauce, pineapple juice, brown sugar or honey, ketchup, rice vinegar, sesame oil, minced garlic, grated ginger, and black pepper until well combined. This will be your marinade for the veggie skewers.
2. Marinate the Vegetables:
    - Place the assorted vegetables in a large shallow dish or a resealable plastic bag.

- Pour the Huli Huli marinade over the vegetables, making sure they are evenly coated. Cover the dish or seal the bag, and refrigerate for at least 30 minutes to allow the flavors to meld.

3. Assemble the Skewers:
    - Preheat your grill to medium-high heat.
    - Thread the marinated vegetables onto the soaked wooden skewers, alternating between different vegetables for variety and color.
4. Grill the Skewers:
    - Lightly oil the grill grates to prevent sticking.
    - Place the assembled veggie skewers on the preheated grill.
    - Grill for 8-10 minutes, turning occasionally, or until the vegetables are tender and lightly charred.
5. Serve:
    - Remove the grilled Huli Huli veggie skewers from the grill and transfer them to a serving platter.
    - Garnish with chopped green onions and sesame seeds, if desired, for added flavor and presentation.
    - Serve the skewers hot as a delicious and nutritious vegetarian main dish or side.

These Huli Huli veggie skewers are bursting with tropical flavors and make a delightful addition to any summer BBQ or outdoor gathering. Enjoy the sweet and savory goodness of grilled vegetables with this Hawaiian-inspired dish!

Mango Coconut Ice Cream

Ingredients:

- 2 ripe mangoes, peeled and diced (about 2 cups)
- 1 (13.5 oz) can full-fat coconut milk
- 1/2 cup granulated sugar (adjust to taste)
- 1 teaspoon vanilla extract
- Pinch of salt
- Optional: Toasted coconut flakes or chopped nuts for garnish

Instructions:

1. Prepare the Mango Puree:
    - Place the diced mangoes in a blender or food processor and blend until smooth to make mango puree. Set aside.
2. Make the Ice Cream Base:
    - In a large mixing bowl, combine the coconut milk, granulated sugar, vanilla extract, and a pinch of salt. Whisk until the sugar is completely dissolved.
3. Combine the Mango Puree with the Ice Cream Base:
    - Add the mango puree to the coconut milk mixture and whisk until well combined.
4. Chill the Mixture:
    - Cover the bowl with plastic wrap or a lid and refrigerate the mixture for at least 2-4 hours, or until thoroughly chilled. Chilling the mixture helps improve the texture of the ice cream.
5. Churn the Ice Cream:
    - Once the mixture is chilled, pour it into an ice cream maker and churn according to the manufacturer's instructions until it reaches a soft-serve consistency.
6. Transfer to Freezer Container:
    - Transfer the churned ice cream to a freezer-safe container, smoothing the top with a spatula.
7. Freeze until Firm:
    - Cover the container with a lid or plastic wrap and freeze the ice cream for at least 4-6 hours, or until it is firm and scoopable.
8. Serve:
    - When ready to serve, let the ice cream sit at room temperature for a few minutes to soften slightly.
    - Scoop the mango coconut ice cream into bowls or cones.

- Garnish with toasted coconut flakes or chopped nuts, if desired, for added texture and flavor.
9. Enjoy:
    - Serve and enjoy this creamy and refreshing mango coconut ice cream!

This homemade mango coconut ice cream is perfect for cooling off on hot summer days or as a sweet treat any time of the year. The combination of tropical flavors is sure to be a hit with everyone!

Pineapple Teriyaki Veggie Burgers

Ingredients:

For the Veggie Burgers:

- 2 cups cooked quinoa or brown rice
- 1 (15 oz) can black beans, drained and rinsed
- 1 cup finely chopped mushrooms
- 1/2 cup finely chopped red bell pepper
- 1/4 cup finely chopped red onion
- 2 cloves garlic, minced
- 1 tablespoon soy sauce or tamari
- 1 teaspoon ground cumin
- 1/2 teaspoon smoked paprika
- Salt and pepper to taste
- 1/4 cup breadcrumbs or oat flour
- 1 tablespoon vegetable oil for cooking

For the Teriyaki Sauce:

- 1/4 cup soy sauce or tamari
- 2 tablespoons brown sugar or honey
- 2 tablespoons rice vinegar
- 1 tablespoon mirin (Japanese rice wine) or dry sherry
- 1 clove garlic, minced
- 1 teaspoon grated ginger
- 1 teaspoon cornstarch mixed with 1 tablespoon water (optional, for thickening)

For Assembling:

- Burger buns
- Grilled pineapple slices
- Lettuce leaves
- Sliced red onion
- Sliced avocado
- Sriracha mayo or teriyaki sauce (optional, for extra flavor)

Instructions:

1. Prepare the Veggie Burger Patties:
   - In a large mixing bowl, mash the black beans with a fork or potato masher until mostly smooth.
   - Add cooked quinoa or brown rice, chopped mushrooms, chopped red bell pepper, chopped red onion, minced garlic, soy sauce, ground cumin, smoked paprika, salt, and pepper. Mix until well combined.
   - Stir in the breadcrumbs or oat flour until the mixture holds together.
   - Divide the mixture into equal portions and shape them into burger patties.
2. Make the Teriyaki Sauce:
   - In a small saucepan, combine soy sauce, brown sugar or honey, rice vinegar, mirin or dry sherry, minced garlic, and grated ginger.
   - Bring the mixture to a simmer over medium heat, stirring occasionally.
   - If you prefer a thicker sauce, add the cornstarch-water mixture to the sauce and cook for an additional 1-2 minutes until thickened. Remove from heat and set aside.
3. Cook the Veggie Burgers:
   - Heat vegetable oil in a skillet or grill pan over medium heat.
   - Cook the veggie burger patties for 4-5 minutes on each side, or until golden brown and heated through.
4. Grill the Pineapple Slices:
   - Lightly oil the grill grates or grill pan.
   - Grill the pineapple slices for 2-3 minutes on each side, or until grill marks form and the pineapple is caramelized.
5. Assemble the Burgers:
   - Toast the burger buns if desired.
   - Place a lettuce leaf on the bottom half of each bun.
   - Top with a veggie burger patty, grilled pineapple slice, sliced red onion, and sliced avocado.
   - Drizzle with teriyaki sauce or sriracha mayo if desired.
   - Place the top half of the bun on each assembled burger.
6. Serve:
   - Serve the pineapple teriyaki veggie burgers immediately, and enjoy this delicious and flavorful vegetarian meal!

These pineapple teriyaki veggie burgers are packed with savory and sweet flavors, making them a satisfying and mouthwatering meal option for vegetarians and meat-eaters alike.

Hawaiian Chicken Salad

Ingredients:

For the Salad:

- 2 cups cooked chicken breast, shredded or diced
- 1 cup pineapple chunks, fresh or canned, drained
- 1 cup grapes, halved
- 1/2 cup shredded coconut
- 1/4 cup sliced almonds or macadamia nuts
- 1/4 cup diced red onion
- 1/4 cup diced celery
- 2 green onions, thinly sliced
- Fresh cilantro or parsley for garnish (optional)

For the Dressing:

- 1/2 cup mayonnaise
- 2 tablespoons Greek yogurt or sour cream
- 1 tablespoon honey or maple syrup
- 1 tablespoon lime juice
- 1 teaspoon soy sauce or tamari
- Salt and pepper to taste

Instructions:

1. Prepare the Dressing:
    - In a small bowl, whisk together the mayonnaise, Greek yogurt or sour cream, honey or maple syrup, lime juice, soy sauce or tamari, salt, and pepper until smooth. Adjust the seasoning to taste.
2. Assemble the Salad:
    - In a large mixing bowl, combine the cooked chicken breast, pineapple chunks, halved grapes, shredded coconut, sliced almonds or macadamia nuts, diced red onion, diced celery, and thinly sliced green onions.
3. Add the Dressing:
    - Pour the prepared dressing over the salad ingredients in the mixing bowl.
4. Toss to Combine:
    - Gently toss all the ingredients together until well coated with the dressing.

5. Chill:
    - Cover the bowl with plastic wrap or transfer the salad to a sealed container.
    - Refrigerate the Hawaiian chicken salad for at least 30 minutes to allow the flavors to meld and the salad to chill.
6. Garnish and Serve:
    - Before serving, garnish the Hawaiian chicken salad with fresh cilantro or parsley, if desired, for a pop of color and freshness.
    - Serve the salad chilled as a delicious and refreshing meal or side dish.

Enjoy this Hawaiian chicken salad as a light and satisfying meal, perfect for lunch or dinner on warm summer days! The combination of tender chicken, tropical fruits, and creamy dressing is sure to be a hit with family and friends.

Taro Bubble Tea

Ingredients:

- 1/4 cup taro powder
- 1 cup hot water
- 2 tablespoons sugar (adjust to taste)
- 1/2 cup cooked tapioca pearls (boba)
- 1 cup ice cubes
- 1/2 cup milk (you can use dairy or non-dairy milk like almond milk)
- Optional: honey or condensed milk for added sweetness
- Optional: taro-flavored syrup for extra flavor

Instructions:

1. In a small bowl, mix the taro powder and hot water until the powder is completely dissolved. Add sugar to the taro mixture and stir until dissolved. Let it cool to room temperature.
2. Cook the tapioca pearls according to the package instructions. Once cooked, rinse them under cold water and drain.
3. In a blender, combine the cooled taro mixture, ice cubes, milk, and any optional sweeteners or flavorings (such as honey, condensed milk, or taro syrup).
4. Blend the mixture until smooth and creamy. Taste and adjust sweetness as desired by adding more sugar or sweetener.
5. Place a few cooked tapioca pearls (boba) into the bottom of a glass or cup.
6. Pour the blended taro mixture over the tapioca pearls.
7. Insert a bubble tea straw and give it a gentle stir to combine the flavors.
8. Serve immediately and enjoy your homemade Taro Bubble Tea!

Feel free to adjust the sweetness and consistency of the bubble tea according to your preferences. You can also customize it by adding toppings like whipped cream or coconut flakes for extra flair!

Coconut Tapioca Pudding

Ingredients:

- 1/2 cup small pearl tapioca
- 2 cups coconut milk
- 1/2 cup sugar
- 1/4 teaspoon salt
- 1 teaspoon vanilla extract
- Optional toppings: sliced mango, diced pineapple, shredded coconut, or whipped cream

Instructions:

1. Rinse the tapioca pearls under cold water in a fine-mesh strainer for a couple of minutes. Drain well.
2. In a medium saucepan, combine the drained tapioca pearls, coconut milk, sugar, and salt.
3. Let the mixture sit for 15-30 minutes to allow the tapioca pearls to soften slightly.
4. After soaking, place the saucepan over medium heat and bring the mixture to a gentle simmer, stirring constantly to prevent sticking.
5. Once the mixture begins to simmer, reduce the heat to low and continue to cook, stirring frequently, for about 15-20 minutes, or until the tapioca pearls are translucent and tender.
6. Remove the saucepan from the heat and stir in the vanilla extract.
7. Let the pudding cool slightly before transferring it to individual serving dishes or a large serving bowl.
8. Cover the pudding with plastic wrap, pressing it directly onto the surface of the pudding to prevent a skin from forming.
9. Refrigerate the pudding for at least 1-2 hours, or until chilled and set.
10. Before serving, give the pudding a gentle stir. If desired, top each serving with sliced mango, diced pineapple, shredded coconut, or a dollop of whipped cream.
11. Enjoy your creamy and delicious Coconut Tapioca Pudding!

This pudding is best enjoyed chilled and can be stored in the refrigerator for up to 3-4 days. Feel free to adjust the sweetness according to your taste preferences by adding more or less sugar.

Hawaiian Breakfast Sandwich

Ingredients:

- 4 slices of Hawaiian sweet bread or King's Hawaiian rolls
- 4 slices of cooked ham
- 4 slices of pineapple (fresh or canned)
- 4 slices of Swiss cheese
- 4 large eggs
- Salt and pepper to taste
- Butter or cooking spray

Instructions:

1. Preheat your oven to 350°F (175°C).
2. If using canned pineapple slices, drain them well. If using fresh pineapple, slice it into 1/2-inch thick rounds and remove the core.
3. Heat a skillet over medium heat and lightly grease it with butter or cooking spray.
4. Crack the eggs into the skillet and cook them to your desired doneness (fried or scrambled). Season with salt and pepper to taste.
5. While the eggs are cooking, split the Hawaiian sweet bread or rolls and place them on a baking sheet.
6. Layer each bottom half of the bread with a slice of ham, followed by a slice of pineapple, a slice of Swiss cheese, and finally, a cooked egg.
7. Top each sandwich with the remaining bread halves.
8. Transfer the baking sheet to the preheated oven and bake for about 5-7 minutes, or until the cheese is melted and the bread is lightly toasted.
9. Remove the sandwiches from the oven and let them cool slightly before serving.
10. Slice the sandwiches in half and enjoy your Hawaiian Breakfast Sandwich with a taste of the islands!

Feel free to customize your sandwich by adding other ingredients like bacon, avocado, or a drizzle of teriyaki sauce for extra flavor. Serve it alongside fresh fruit or a side of hash browns for a complete breakfast meal.

Haupia Pie

Ingredients for Crust:

- 1 1/2 cups graham cracker crumbs
- 1/4 cup granulated sugar
- 6 tablespoons melted butter

Ingredients for Haupia Filling:

- 1 (13.5 oz) can coconut milk
- 1 cup whole milk
- 1/2 cup granulated sugar
- 1/2 cup cornstarch
- 1/4 teaspoon salt

Ingredients for Whipped Cream Topping:

- 1 cup heavy cream
- 2 tablespoons powdered sugar
- 1 teaspoon vanilla extract

Instructions:

1. Preheat your oven to 350°F (175°C).
2. In a mixing bowl, combine the graham cracker crumbs, granulated sugar, and melted butter. Mix until well combined.
3. Press the crumb mixture into a 9-inch pie dish, covering the bottom and sides evenly to form the crust.
4. Bake the crust in the preheated oven for about 8-10 minutes, or until lightly golden brown. Remove from the oven and let it cool completely.
5. In a saucepan, combine the coconut milk, whole milk, granulated sugar, cornstarch, and salt for the haupia filling. Whisk until smooth.
6. Place the saucepan over medium heat and cook the mixture, stirring constantly, until it thickens and comes to a gentle boil, about 5-7 minutes.
7. Once the mixture has thickened, remove it from the heat and pour it into the cooled graham cracker crust.

8. Smooth the top of the haupia filling with a spatula and let it cool to room temperature. Then, refrigerate the pie for at least 2-3 hours, or until set.
9. In a mixing bowl, whip the heavy cream, powdered sugar, and vanilla extract together until stiff peaks form.
10. Spread the whipped cream over the chilled haupia filling, covering the entire surface of the pie.
11. Optional: Garnish the pie with toasted coconut flakes or shaved chocolate for extra flavor and decoration.
12. Slice and serve your delicious Haupia Pie chilled, and enjoy this tropical treat with friends and family!

This creamy and coconutty dessert is perfect for any occasion, and it captures the essence of Hawaiian cuisine with its rich flavors and smooth texture.

Pineapple Coconut Cake

Ingredients for Cake:

- 2 cups all-purpose flour
- 1 1/2 cups granulated sugar
- 1 teaspoon baking powder
- 1/2 teaspoon baking soda
- 1/4 teaspoon salt
- 1 cup crushed pineapple (drained)
- 1/2 cup unsweetened shredded coconut
- 3/4 cup vegetable oil
- 3 large eggs
- 1 teaspoon vanilla extract

Ingredients for Coconut Cream Cheese Frosting:

- 8 oz (1 package) cream cheese, softened
- 1/2 cup unsalted butter, softened
- 4 cups powdered sugar
- 1 teaspoon vanilla extract
- 1/2 cup unsweetened shredded coconut (for garnish)

Instructions:

1. Preheat your oven to 350°F (175°C). Grease and flour two 9-inch round cake pans.
2. In a large mixing bowl, whisk together the flour, sugar, baking powder, baking soda, and salt until well combined.
3. Add the crushed pineapple (make sure to drain excess juice) and shredded coconut to the dry ingredients, and mix until evenly distributed.
4. In a separate bowl, whisk together the vegetable oil, eggs, and vanilla extract until smooth.
5. Pour the wet ingredients into the dry ingredients and stir until just combined. Be careful not to overmix.
6. Divide the batter evenly between the prepared cake pans and smooth the tops with a spatula.
7. Bake in the preheated oven for 25-30 minutes, or until a toothpick inserted into the center comes out clean.

8. Remove the cakes from the oven and let them cool in the pans for 10 minutes before transferring them to a wire rack to cool completely.
9. While the cakes are cooling, prepare the coconut cream cheese frosting. In a mixing bowl, beat the softened cream cheese and butter together until smooth and creamy.
10. Gradually add the powdered sugar and vanilla extract, and continue beating until the frosting is light and fluffy.
11. Once the cakes are completely cool, place one cake layer on a serving plate or cake stand. Spread a layer of frosting on top.
12. Place the second cake layer on top and frost the top and sides of the cake with the remaining frosting.
13. Optional: Press shredded coconut onto the sides of the cake for decoration and extra coconut flavor.
14. Chill the cake in the refrigerator for at least 30 minutes before serving to allow the frosting to set.
15. Slice and serve your delicious Pineapple Coconut Cake, and enjoy the tropical flavors!

This cake is perfect for special occasions or as a delightful dessert to enjoy with family and friends. The combination of pineapple and coconut creates a refreshing and irresistible flavor that will transport you to the tropics with every bite.

Ahi Poke Nachos

Ingredients:

- 1 lb sushi-grade ahi tuna, diced into small cubes
- 1/4 cup soy sauce
- 1 tablespoon sesame oil
- 1 teaspoon rice vinegar
- 1 teaspoon honey or agave nectar
- 1 teaspoon Sriracha sauce (adjust to taste)
- 2 green onions, thinly sliced
- 1 avocado, diced
- 1/4 cup diced cucumber
- 1/4 cup diced mango
- 1/4 cup diced red onion
- 1/4 cup chopped cilantro
- 1 tablespoon sesame seeds
- Tortilla chips (for serving)

Instructions:

1. In a mixing bowl, combine the soy sauce, sesame oil, rice vinegar, honey or agave nectar, and Sriracha sauce to make the marinade.
2. Add the diced ahi tuna to the marinade and gently toss to coat. Cover the bowl and refrigerate for at least 30 minutes to allow the flavors to meld.
3. While the tuna is marinating, prepare the toppings. Combine the sliced green onions, diced avocado, cucumber, mango, red onion, and chopped cilantro in separate bowls.
4. After the tuna has marinated, remove it from the refrigerator and drain off any excess marinade.
5. Arrange the tortilla chips on a large serving platter or individual plates.
6. Spoon the marinated ahi tuna over the tortilla chips, spreading it out evenly.
7. Scatter the prepared toppings over the tuna, including the diced avocado, cucumber, mango, red onion, green onions, and cilantro.
8. Sprinkle sesame seeds over the top for added flavor and texture.
9. Serve the Ahi Poke Nachos immediately, and enjoy this delicious and refreshing appetizer!

These Ahi Poke Nachos are perfect for parties, gatherings, or as a flavorful snack any time of the day. The combination of fresh ahi tuna, vibrant toppings, and crispy tortilla chips creates a dish that is both visually stunning and incredibly tasty. Adjust the toppings and seasoning according to your taste preferences, and enjoy the burst of flavors with each bite!

Taro Pancakes with Coconut Syrup

Ingredients for Taro Pancakes:

- 1 cup taro root, cooked and mashed (you can use fresh taro or taro powder)
- 1 cup all-purpose flour
- 2 tablespoons granulated sugar
- 1 teaspoon baking powder
- 1/4 teaspoon salt
- 1 cup milk (dairy or non-dairy)
- 1 large egg
- 2 tablespoons melted butter or vegetable oil
- Butter or oil for cooking

Ingredients for Coconut Syrup:

- 1 cup coconut milk
- 1 cup granulated sugar
- 1/4 teaspoon vanilla extract
- Pinch of salt

Instructions:

1. If using fresh taro root, peel and dice the taro into small pieces. Boil or steam the taro until tender, then mash it until smooth. If using taro powder, prepare according to the package instructions and let it cool.
2. In a large mixing bowl, combine the mashed taro, flour, sugar, baking powder, and salt.
3. In a separate bowl, whisk together the milk, egg, and melted butter or oil.
4. Pour the wet ingredients into the dry ingredients and stir until just combined. Be careful not to overmix; a few lumps are okay.
5. Heat a skillet or griddle over medium heat and lightly grease it with butter or oil.
6. Pour a ladleful of batter onto the hot skillet to form each pancake. Cook until bubbles form on the surface of the pancakes and the edges look set, then flip and cook until golden brown on the other side.
7. Transfer the cooked pancakes to a plate and keep warm while you prepare the coconut syrup.

8. To make the coconut syrup, combine the coconut milk, sugar, vanilla extract, and salt in a small saucepan. Bring to a simmer over medium heat, stirring occasionally.
9. Let the syrup simmer for about 5-7 minutes, or until slightly thickened.
10. Remove the syrup from the heat and let it cool slightly before serving.
11. Drizzle the warm coconut syrup over the taro pancakes and serve immediately.
12. Enjoy your delicious Taro Pancakes with Coconut Syrup for a taste of tropical paradise!

These pancakes are fluffy, flavorful, and perfect for a special breakfast or brunch. The addition of taro adds a unique twist, while the homemade coconut syrup adds a touch of sweetness and indulgence. Serve the pancakes with fresh fruit or whipped cream for an extra treat!

Hawaiian Macaroni Salad

Ingredients:

- 8 oz elbow macaroni
- 1/2 cup mayonnaise
- 1/4 cup whole milk
- 2 tablespoons apple cider vinegar
- 1 tablespoon granulated sugar
- 1/2 teaspoon salt
- 1/4 teaspoon black pepper
- 1/2 cup grated carrot
- 1/2 cup grated onion
- 1/4 cup chopped green onions (scallions), plus extra for garnish
- Optional: cooked ham or crispy bacon, diced (for added flavor)

Instructions:

1. Cook the elbow macaroni according to the package instructions until al dente. Drain the cooked macaroni and rinse it under cold water to stop the cooking process. Drain well and transfer to a large mixing bowl.
2. In a separate bowl, whisk together the mayonnaise, milk, apple cider vinegar, sugar, salt, and black pepper until smooth and well combined.
3. Pour the dressing over the cooked macaroni in the mixing bowl. Add the grated carrot, grated onion, and chopped green onions (scallions) to the bowl.
4. Optional: Add diced cooked ham or crispy bacon to the bowl for added flavor and texture.
5. Gently toss all the ingredients together until the macaroni is evenly coated with the dressing and the vegetables are distributed throughout.
6. Cover the bowl with plastic wrap and refrigerate the macaroni salad for at least 1-2 hours, or until chilled.
7. Before serving, give the macaroni salad a final stir. If the salad seems a bit dry after chilling, you can add a splash of milk to loosen it up.
8. Garnish the macaroni salad with additional chopped green onions (scallions) for extra freshness and flavor.
9. Serve the Hawaiian Macaroni Salad as a side dish at your next barbecue, potluck, or luau, and enjoy its creamy, tangy goodness!

This Hawaiian-style macaroni salad is creamy, tangy, and packed with flavor. The combination of mayonnaise, vinegar, and sugar creates a unique dressing that perfectly complements the tender macaroni and crunchy vegetables. It's a classic side dish that pairs well with grilled meats, seafood, or simply enjoyed on its own.

Lū'au Punch

Ingredients:

- 4 cups pineapple juice
- 2 cups orange juice
- 1 cup guava juice
- 1/4 cup lime juice (freshly squeezed)
- 2 cups lemon-lime soda or ginger ale
- 1/2 cup grenadine syrup
- Pineapple slices, orange slices, and maraschino cherries for garnish
- Ice cubes

Instructions:

1. In a large punch bowl or pitcher, combine the pineapple juice, orange juice, guava juice, and lime juice.
2. Stir in the grenadine syrup until well combined. The grenadine will add a lovely pink hue to the punch.
3. Just before serving, pour in the lemon-lime soda or ginger ale to add a fizzy element to the punch. Stir gently to combine.
4. Add ice cubes to the punch bowl or individual glasses to keep the punch chilled.
5. Garnish the punch with pineapple slices, orange slices, and maraschino cherries for a festive touch.
6. Serve the Lū'au Punch immediately and enjoy the tropical flavors!

This Lū'au Punch is a refreshing and fruity beverage that captures the essence of the Hawaiian islands. The combination of pineapple, orange, guava, and lime juices creates a delightful flavor profile that is both sweet and tangy. The addition of grenadine syrup adds a pop of color, while the fizzy soda or ginger ale adds a refreshing effervescence. It's the perfect drink to sip on a hot day or to serve at your next luau or summer party!

Grilled Pineapple Slices with Cinnamon Sugar

Ingredients:

- 1 ripe pineapple, peeled and cored
- 1/4 cup granulated sugar
- 1 teaspoon ground cinnamon
- Cooking spray or vegetable oil for grilling

Instructions:

1. Preheat your grill to medium-high heat.
2. In a small bowl, mix together the granulated sugar and ground cinnamon until well combined to make the cinnamon sugar mixture.
3. Slice the pineapple into rings, about 1/2 to 3/4 inch thick.
4. Lightly coat both sides of each pineapple slice with cooking spray or brush with vegetable oil to prevent sticking on the grill.
5. Sprinkle the cinnamon sugar mixture evenly over both sides of each pineapple slice, pressing gently to adhere.
6. Place the pineapple slices directly onto the preheated grill grates.
7. Grill the pineapple slices for about 2-3 minutes per side, or until grill marks form and the pineapple is heated through.
8. Remove the grilled pineapple slices from the grill and transfer them to a serving platter.
9. Serve the grilled pineapple slices warm as a delicious dessert or snack.
10. Optionally, you can sprinkle additional cinnamon sugar over the grilled pineapple slices before serving for extra sweetness and flavor.

Enjoy these grilled pineapple slices with cinnamon sugar as a delightful and refreshing treat that's perfect for summer barbecues, picnics, or any time you're craving something sweet with a hint of smoky flavor from the grill!

Hawaiian Shaved Ice with Tropical Fruit Syrup

Ingredients for Shaved Ice:

- Ice cubes or shaved ice (you can use a shaved ice machine or crush ice in a blender)
- Assorted tropical fruits for topping (such as pineapple, mango, kiwi, passion fruit, or papaya)
- Sweetened condensed milk (optional, for drizzling)

Ingredients for Tropical Fruit Syrup:

- 1 cup chopped mixed tropical fruits (pineapple, mango, kiwi, etc.)
- 1/2 cup granulated sugar
- 1/2 cup water
- Juice of 1 lime or lemon

Instructions:

1. Prepare the Tropical Fruit Syrup: In a small saucepan, combine the chopped mixed tropical fruits, granulated sugar, water, and lime or lemon juice.
2. Bring the mixture to a simmer over medium heat, stirring occasionally until the sugar is dissolved.
3. Once the sugar is dissolved, reduce the heat to low and let the syrup simmer for about 10-15 minutes, or until the fruit is soft and the syrup has thickened slightly.
4. Remove the syrup from the heat and let it cool slightly. Then, strain the syrup through a fine-mesh sieve to remove any fruit solids, pressing down on the fruit to extract as much liquid as possible. Discard the solids.
5. Transfer the strained syrup to a jar or bowl and let it cool completely. You can store any leftover syrup in the refrigerator for up to a week.
6. Prepare the Shaved Ice: If you're using ice cubes, place them in a blender and pulse until finely crushed. If you have a shaved ice machine, use it to create fluffy shaved ice.
7. Scoop the shaved ice into serving bowls or cups.
8. Drizzle the cooled Tropical Fruit Syrup over the shaved ice.
9. Top the shaved ice with assorted tropical fruits, such as diced pineapple, mango slices, kiwi slices, passion fruit pulp, or papaya chunks.

10. Optionally, drizzle sweetened condensed milk over the top for added creaminess and sweetness.
11. Serve the Hawaiian Shaved Ice with Tropical Fruit Syrup immediately and enjoy the refreshing and tropical flavors!

This Hawaiian Shaved Ice with Tropical Fruit Syrup is a delightful and refreshing dessert that's sure to cool you down on hot summer days. The combination of fluffy shaved ice, sweet and tangy fruit syrup, and assorted tropical fruits creates a burst of tropical flavors in every bite. It's a fun and customizable dessert that you can enjoy with friends and family at any summer gathering or luau-themed party!

www.ingramcontent.com/pod-product-compliance
Lightning Source LLC
LaVergne TN
LVHW081607060526
838201LV00054B/2128